There's Always Hope

T Lee Sizemore

This is a work of fiction.

Text is copyrighted by

T Lee Sizemore, DVM, RN ©2017

Library of Congress Control Number: 2017916315

All rights reserved.

No part of this book may be

reproduced, transmitted, or stored in an information retrieval

system in any form or by any means,

graphic, electronic, or mechanical without prior written

permission from the author.

First Edition 2016

Printed in the United States of America

A 2 Z Press LLC

PO Box 582

Deleon Springs, FL 32130

bestlittleonlinebookstore.com

bestlittleonlinebookstore@gmail.com

386-681-7402

ISBN: 978-1-946908-90-2

Dedication

This book is dedicated in memory
of my beloved grandfather,
Alexander Balcziunas.

INTRODUCTION

There's Always Hope is a short, but important look at the effects of divorce on young children.

This book is a work of fiction, however, it is based on actual events in a young girl's life whose parents divorced when she was just five years old.

This book takes the reader through Hope's journey from the divorce through her young years into her teens to her college graduation. Hope tells how she felt inside and the struggles she faced.

It is the hope of the author that parents, stepparents, children, and family and others involved with the children be aware of how all the events surrounding a divorce impact the children.

Most children are unable to express deep feelings and often blame themselves for the decisions the adults in their lives make. This can lead to emotional confusion for many years and sometimes even the life of the child.

Help is available for children of divorce. Most importantly, the parents should be aware, mature, and attend to the deep needs of their children. The author knows how difficult this can be because of the trauma they face personally in a divorce situation, however, we can all weather our storms together.

Chapter 1

Hope moved closer to the mirror as she puckered her lips and patted them with tissue, making sure her lipstick covered them perfectly and evenly. She turned her head from side to side admiring the natural-looking blush on her cheeks and blue eye shadow bringing out the beauty in her sky-blue eyes. Her strawberry blonde hair was pulled back and up to fit under the graduation cap sitting on her lap; waiting to worn in just minutes.

Needing to escape the overwhelming aroma of perfume and hair spray, Hope slipped off her stool and pushed her way through the crowd of girls gathered close to the mirrors in the prep room.

Graduation was a big day for everyone. Hope watched the other girls fixing hair and putting the finishing touches on makeup. The girls laughed as they shared their plans for the days following graduation. Everyone had family in to help celebrate and finalize details of the next steps in life.

Hope was also graduating college today. This was a huge milestone in her life. She was quieter than usual, reflecting on each detail of the events of the day. She had always wanted to be a teacher and now she was on the verge of an accomplishment that would allow her to live out her dreams. She walked past the other students to the stage where everyone would stand to receive their diplomas. As Hope poked her head between the curtains, she stood motionless, making sure she imprinted this moment in her memory forever.

Rows of chairs covered the grassy area in front of the stage where the students would sit awaiting their call to receive their diplomas. The sun was bright in the cloudless sky. The gently blowing breeze was nature's perfect gift for today's events.

Parents, grandparents, siblings, and friends gathered to sit patiently waiting for their particular student to receive their honor that day. Hope could hear the marching band practicing for the final events of the day. She saw her father in the last row. He didn't notice her as he held his new wife's hand and talked to people seated next to him. On the other side of the spectator area, Hope noticed her mother, grandmother, and many of her relatives. She knew how proud they were.

Hope reached into the pocket of her dress, a dress now hidden under the ceremonial gown. Her gown matched all the other students. She smiled as she looked down at the gold cross she took from her pocket. She turned it over to read the inscription: "all things are possible." A sadness came over her as she looked again to see if the woman who had given her this cross so many years ago had come to see her graduate.

"Hi, Hope."

"Hi," Hope snapped back. She couldn't see who it was saying 'hello' because they walked by so quickly.

The truth was Hope was oblivious to the sounds of equipment moving on the stage and the laughter and talk between the students of upcoming parties and future plans. She stepped forward a step to look over the crowd of gathering spectators. "Please come," she whispered to herself. Katie was the woman she wanted to see in the seats.

Hope sent Katie her the invitation many months ago, so she would have time to plan her work around the graduation ceremony. Hope was flooded with all the many memories of Katie and she shared. Once Katie told her that was why they are called memories- "so we could both remember the moments we shared forever."

As Hope stood motionless, her mind drifted back in time to a far, faraway place. Many years ago, her parents divorced. Hope remembered that time as if were yesterday.

I was only five. I would lie on my bed hidden away in my upstairs bedroom. My faithful dog, Jasmine, would come with me wherever I went. With one hand, I stroked her soft yellow head and with the other, I twirled my hair. The sound of the wind whistled through the leaves of the enormous oak tree standing outside the front windows. Down below were the sounds of the neighborhood. Sounds of lawn mowers humming across front yards filled my window. Sprinklers watered purple, red, and yellow flowers in the yard across the street. Boys next door were hitting balls and yelling, "Come batter, batter, batter, batter," to each other. Then I heard them pretending to be fire trucks and imitating the siren on the truck. Sounds of joggers saying, "Hello" to neighbors and big wheel riders along the sidewalk were also familiar sounds to me. Even as these happy sounds below filled my window, they did not comfort me.

I made a pretend world. This was the world where nothing hurt. In my pretend world, my mom and dad did not fight, they loved each other and we were a family and did all the things I watched other families doing. In this world, we walked in the park, laughed and hugged. We went for ice cream and on family vacations. I would pretend Dad would come home from work, and after Mom made supper, we all sat at the table and ate like a family. We visited relatives on holidays together. No matter how hard I tried to stay in my make-believe world, it was always interrupted by shouting and slamming doors as my parents fought. They yelled at each other for hours it seemed.

My real world was one of much uncertainty. I was full of turmoil and felt such helplessness to fix what was wrong. What made me think at such a young age that I could fix all this? I was hurting in a way I could not express at my young age. I loved them both and wanted them to stay in the same house. Mom was always leaving. Where would she go? Where would I go? Who would still take care of me? Would Dad also leave me? I didn't think Mom would ever leave. I was always afraid of the worst things that could happen. It would be many years before I would develop the emotional and mental skills to sort all these things out.

I did not realize it then, but I see clearly now that my world should have been filled with swimming, swinging, playing ball and dolls. It should have been spent learning to be a child and having friends. I should have learned to play the violin or piano or other instrument, had sleepovers and birthday parties. Instead, I was consumed with fear and hurt. Something was very wrong in my family and I could not find a way to keep the two people I loved so much together. I was sad and spent most of my time trying to figure out how to fix my broken life. There was no carefree childhood here for me. I would learn later of the lost childhood that I was experiencing.

I did not know the words to tell them that my heart was breaking into a million pieces since I didn't have a way to express my thoughts and feelings. I couldn't find anyone to talk to. I wished I knew the words to match the very disturbing feelings inside me. No one seemed to know the words to say to me either. They didn't seem to see the hurt. The hurt was deep inside of me. It was as deep as it could go. They must have thought I was not affected by their fighting and threats of divorce. They were wrong.

I worried all day long. I could not concentrate like the other kids in my classroom. They seemed so happy and carefree and they were there to enjoy the day and learn. I was worried about what was happening at home. I was worried if I would still have a family when I arrived home. What I didn't know at this time was that I was consumed with big person problems instead of the problems and happiness of childhood.

Even when the house was quiet, Mom would sit in the kitchen and Dad sat in the front room. There was so much sadness there. Most of the time I wished I were still a baby. When I was just a baby, we were a family and they would take me to relatives' houses for Christmas and birthdays. Sometimes we did things like other families. They were a couple then. We were a family then.

My mom and dad fought again and again. As they yelled at each other, I remember pulling at my mom's shirt and silently begging her to stay. She yelled at my dad once more, pushed my hands away from her shirt, and walked out the door. I heard it slam. I heard her start her car and pull out of the driveway. We were left alone. My dad was crushed as I. Dad and I didn't talk. The house was quiet now. What did this mean? The worst had happened. They divorced. My world as I knew it came to an end. I could think of no greater blow.

"Hey, Hope, are you ready to get that diploma and walk out into the great big world today?" Hope heard Dave's voice behind her.

Her memories would have to take a short break as she hugged him and wished him well.

"Today's the big day," Hope said.

Chapter 2

As the Crowd continued to gather, Hope's mind again drifted back off to the distant past.

Two years after Mon and Dan divorced, things were still very difficult. Mom left. Dad and I had a routine. We did the same things each day, but we were still two brokenhearted people. I was seven now.

I now had two lives in two homes. Shared custody. I spent weekdays at Dad's and weekends at Grandma's. I had two holidays, two birthdays, two sets of clothes, and two sets of rules. It was exhausting. It was not the fun everyone claimed it would be. When I was with my dad, I missed my mom. When I was with my mom, I missed my dad. I obviously could not be in two places at the same time.

I had a dream. It was a dream that one day I would get everything of mine in one house and live a normal life. I would not have to worry about who bought me what item and how I could only share my belongings at that one house. No more competition to give me the best life at one or the other house. No more being asked to love one parent and one home better than the other. Everything good and everything I wanted felt pretend. Everything bad and what I did not want felt real. I kept hoping Mom would come home soon.

My friends with divorced parents lived with their mothers. I lived with my father. They always thought I was lucky because I saw my dad every day and did things with him. I thought they were lucky because they always saw their mothers and I wished for what I did not have also. Sometimes they wanted to spend time with me to be around a dad and I felt myself wanting to be with them to be around a mom. We were trying to find that missing piece of our lives.

Then one day, a woman named Katie came into our lives. Katie had just moved into the neighborhood. She owned horses and stabled them in the same barn as my dad. I liked her immediately. As we all spent time at the barn, we became friends. Katie became very good friends with my dad and me.

There was a kindness about her that drew my heart to her. She was always happy. Her smile spread across her face and she liked me. Even though she was a grown-up, she really liked spending time with children. I could feel it every time I was with her. She was fun and understood what children needed and wanted.

Since Katie had a job that allowed her free time, I spent a lot of time with her. She made me feel so special- like I was the most special and wonderful girl in the world. She had a way about her that made me feel calm and safe inside. Because of this, I looked forward to seeing her every day after school. She was always at the barn.

Dad and I looked like we had survived the divorce, but Katie saw deeper. As she spent time with us, she saw the hurt we still carried. She liked us. Even though she knew things, she didn't say words about it. But she understood it all. She understood my father's life and mine were devastated. She knew I was exhausted trying to take care of my parents when they were clearly taking care of me. She knew what I did not know - I could not fix anything. She understood I missed my mom and wanted my parents back together and my family the way it should be.

Katie also knew my heart was till broken and I frequently reverted to my baby-hood because that was when life was good and my family was a family. She saw I was filled with fear that prevented me from moving on in my growth and development. I was unable to face the world around me. I was filled with conflict with no way to resolve it. Because I was only five when the divorce happened, critical growth in my personality and emotions did not happen. Each child is affected differently by divorce depending on their age and ability to handle stressful situations as well as how the adults in their lives help them.

Katie was smart. She knew I avoided talking about painful things because it was too painful for me. I could not understand the feelings inside of me and I did not know how to express them. I didn't understand myself at this young age. There were too many buried feelings inside of me that I didn't have the skills to cope with. I don't know how Katie knew all this, but it was a good thing she did.

I continued to grow physically and mentally, but emotionally I was stunted. The emotional trauma of the divorce was what contributed to this. Even though I didn't realize it then, Katie did. I'm glad I didn't understand everything then like I do now, I just enjoyed her kindness. I had survived the divorce, but there were scars. No one talked to me about them, they didn't seem to realize what was happing inside of me, but Katie did. She saw I needed someone to give me permission to be a child and that I needed a grown up with me to love me unconditionally. She knew I was scared and she comforted me. One day I would understand what she helped accomplish inside of me. Katie wanted me to eventually have the information I needed to resolve all the issues that were bigger than life for me at my young age. When children face stressful events they do not ask what is wrong with the adults in their lives, they ask what is wrong with them? What did they do? The answer is nothing is wrong with the child. We live in an imperfect world with imperfect people all around us. But this realization would take many years to realize.

The very best thing about Katie was that no matter what she knew, she loved me anyway. She treated me like she never noticed I was in such need and such pain. She treated me like I was the best little girl she had ever known and that I could accomplish wonderful things in my life. She took me where I was- a scared little girl- to where I needed to be- a happy, pain free young adult. This is how I could get to graduation day today. She walked with me day by day through critical years in my life to allow me to heal and grow. She was like a mom to me.

"Almost time now, Hope. Are you ready?" asked her music teacher, Mrs. Vaughn.

"Yes, Mrs. Vaughn. I was just hoping one more guest was coming today," Hope replied.

Hope didn't mind the brief interruptions, she just kept hoping the ceremony would delay long enough for her to find Katie in the quickly gathering crowd.

I still remember those early days with Katie. They were carefree. Sometimes she talked about the syndrome of a lost childhood. She said it was when a child was preoccupied by things other than being a child. Most children who experience this are from broken homes or abuse homes and have difficulties other children do not experience while growing up. Katie said we were about the business of me being a child. She said we would do childish things and I would work on growing up.

The first thing Katie did was to establish trust and friendship. She brought dinner to my house for my father and me. As she celebrated our birthdays and holidays, she made us feel important and cared about. As she became our friend, it became easy for me to be with her and trust her. The better friends we became and the more my dad and I trusted her, the more we did together. As she worked her way into our hearts, she worked her magic. She studied us and learned what we were about and the things we liked.

Katie did fun things with me. She took me to the park to hike, out for ice cream, played hide-and-seek with me and as many neighborhood children as she could invite to play with us. As the grown-up, she knew I needed to learn to have friends and play with other children. Since she bought all the pizza and ice cream, all the kids would gladly play with us. She took time out of her life to spend it with me.

Katie and I hosted parties at holiday times- like we invited everyone we knew to come to a pumpkin-carving party. The neighborhood boys and girls came with their pumpkins and carving tools. We each made a pumpkin. After, we enjoyed cider and treats. All great fun.

As I look back, I can see the patience she had that I took for granted at the time. All the while we played, she worked. She had a mission with me. She was helping me develop. She was slick. I didn't even know she was doing this, but she did. She was building a childhood for me. This would help me have something to pass on to my children in the future.

Not only did she have me socialize with other children, she helped with the schooling I was behind with because of my not paying attention in school. She knew that in the beginning, my attention span was very short. Every five minutes I wanted to do something different, some different project. Katie just followed along. Her kindness and gentleness helped me relax. She either continued with what I chose to do, or gently redirected me back to what we were doing. She understood the anxiety inside me even when I didn't. She stayed calm and took advantage of the few moments I would pay attention at a time. She rode the waves of my emotions.

I could be happy and laughing one minute and then sad and quiet the next. I was quiet when I remembered my hurts over the divorce or missed my mom. Katie could also spot when I became panicky and she would re-route our activities to something less threatening and less stressful for me until I relaxed and she could have me attempt a more difficult activity. Katie just went with the flow and allowed me to progress at my own pace. She gave me the space to come back to her and the job of growing up.

Sometimes we drove in her car for hours. I sat on her lap while she sang to me. My heart felt safe and peaceful during these times. We mixed work with fun.

Also, in the beginning, I frequently reverted to childish behavior. Katie helped me grow out of the baby stage of my life so I could grow and develop like all the other children I was around. Development is a process and when something painful like a divorce interferes with this process, development and growth is disturbed. What stunted my process was the pain I experienced when the divorce happened.

The phases of development are actual tasks each child must accomplish. They are areas of conflict that need to be resolved and one phase must be conquered before one can proceed to the next level of development. The first phase is to learn trust. Next is to find oneself valuable and able to accomplish things. There are many childhood stages. I was very behind.

I experienced much difficulty trusting the world around me because my needs were unmet during the time of conflict between my parents. My parents were good people and they meant me no harm, it was something that happened to me. Katie didn't make me feel like a freak, she just helped me see that I struggled here and this was why. She took me through the stages of development and helped me grow emotionally.

I came to the conclusion that important people in my life did love me even if I did not always feel it. They did not always disappoint me. I came to accept they weren't always perfect. No one is. My father was consistent in his love and care for me. My mother really wanted me to know she loved me too. Even when others criticized my parents, Katie told me their love for me was genuine. It hurt my feelings very badly when people said negative things about my parents. To me they were the best people in the world. They were perfect in my mind.

The task of trusting is usually accomplished before we can even talk, so it is a deep need when we are hurt at this level. Just talking about it helped me to see that I was not weird or impaired. I was just in need of a little more time to learn to trust others. I still have some issues of trust, but I work on these issues every day. I now understand that people in the world are not perfect and they may disappoint me at times. Overall, I have people who love and support me in the world. When I have difficulty becoming attached to things like pets, I re-hash my determined goals to become more trusting. I am sometimes plagued with the fear of them leaving me or disappointing me. One day, I hope to trust more than I ever thought possible.

As I gained more confidence and developed more, I began to do more activities to build my self-esteem. I needed a sense of being proud of myself and realizing I could accomplish things. At first I realized I did not like myself. I told Katie I didn't like myself. She always treated me as though I had much value. She talked about the things I did as if I had accomplished great things when in reality I may have only drawn a new picture. She never seemed to notice when I made a mistake. She didn't over correct my mistakes. She knew that eventually I would figure most things out myself. Eventually it would all come together. She just guided me through the process and times learning.

Since Katie knew what I liked, she very cleverly drew me into activities that were not only fun, but taught me something also. For instance, I loved to bake cookies. She made measuring and mixing fun. We counted and divided cookies to learn some basic math. All the time, being together and having fun. She never missed an opportunity for me to learn.

Katie took me for swimming lessons. She sat and watched the whole time. I looked up at her and she smiled at me- giving me the thumbs up and yelled, "FABULOUS" each time I did even the smallest thing. She made it easy to try difficult things. She also took me for ice skating lessons and dance lessons and craft classes to give me experience in many things. All these things helped build my self-esteem and confidence. I didn't want to run away from life and social situations. I now had more skills to face the challenges of the world.

In addition to the fun activities, we did my homework together. She was determined I would be successful. She could tell when and what I did not understand of my schoolwork. When she discovered something I missed in class, she found ways to teach me. I remember fractions. I did not understand fractions. She got a pie and showed me a 'whole' pie, a 'half' - or 2 halves- a 'quarter,' and so on. She showed me two pies as well. We did the same thing with a bottle of shampoo. She emptied it out to 'half-filled.' She then divided it more and showed me how fractions worked in real life. She did not stop until I understood. If she noticed I was struggling with something, she gave me a break and after a time, went back to the lesson later. She worked on the concept until I understood it.

We played games like scrabble and monopoly. While playing scrabble, Katie wanted me to learn to spell, but knew I could not spell and play by the rules at the same time, so we did not play with rules. Her goal was to have fun. No score meant no winner or loser- just having fun. Clearly she could win, but did not want me to feel like a failure because that was not what the activity was all about. I learned to make words and place them on the board. Stress was minimal and because of this I became better and better at spelling as we continued to play. Not such a bad plan- learning, building self- esteem, and having fun at the same time.

Monopoly was to learn about money and counting money, so we played any way that helped me buy property and build houses and hotels. Katie and I made up our own rules. It would be many years before I realized there were real rules for playing monopoly and scrabble. Katie used these games to help me learn and develop. It worked.

Reading was another challenge I faced. I loved reading and considered it delightful, but could not read when we first met. Even though I couldn't read myself, I loved picture books. Katie spent at least one hour each night before bedtime reading to me. She read to me about Lyle the Crocodile, Curious George, Amelia Bedelia, and others. I saw the words and heard the words over and over. Slowly, she coaxed me to read some of the pages. I wouldn't at first. I was too scared, but as I read, I gained confidence. Soon we were reading chapter books and she would read a chapter and I would read a chapter until I was able to read the entire book.

I remember one night after reading a while, I turned on my back, looked up at the ceiling, folded my hands across my chest, and prayed, "Please let Mommy come back home." Katie watched with sadness in her eyes. Under her breath I think she prayed too, but Mommy never did come back home.

I still had such good memories with Katie though. It was a time that seemed as if the rest of the world didn't exist. I was healing and gaining confidence to do more and more in life. Katie found a neighbor girl to be my best friend. This was a girl anyone would like as a best friend and we did everything together. I learned I could be a friend and I could have good days and bad days and learn to give and take. She liked me, so it helped me like myself a little more too. I began to look at myself as a person of value who could be loved and respected. My introverted nature was opening up. The feelings of wishing I was invisible were leaving me. I was stepping out to new and different social situations each day. I was also becoming more confident in myself even if others were better at some activities than I was. I learned I was good at some things, average at others, and just plain terrible at some things and it was okay. This was also part of my development and would eventually lead to my sense of identity - who I was in the world. Katie told me I would be ready for adulthood and romantic relationships then. I dreamt of a future.

Another important thing Katie did for me was to never compare me to other children. She said that 'comparisons are odious.' This explained meant that comparisons are hateful and abominable. They are the most devastating thing one can do to a child's sense of being. Comparing one child to another made children feel worthless and substandard.

"This was no way for any child to think about themselves," Katie would say.

A child's value is in their being unique and wonderful and precious for just being them, not being based on anything else. One child could never be just like another because each and every child is one-of-a-kind.

All during these times, Katie was careful to protect me from the meanness that other children could be capable of. She protected me any time she could. Everyone knows a certain amount of cruelty from other children happens in a lifetime, but I could see how it upset her when I was the innocent victim of another child's insensitivity. Katie felt that one day I would be able to let it all roll off my back, but as a small hurting child, I was fragile. She felt that it would cause me unnecessary hurt and that I had had enough hurt already for my young age. Even though mean things seem to be a part of growing up, she made certain they were as minimal as possible. I now realize how she picked kind children to spend time with me. She was building me up before the challenges of life would test my inner strength.

It was a lot of work to get through those years, but Katie never gave up on me. These were critical areas and as I accomplished these deep areas of needed development, she always let me go at my own speed. She was my safety net when I needed one. I was so lucky to have such a friend to take my hand and walk with me through these years of my journey in life.

It would take me many years to appreciate this woman. This was only half of what she actually did for me and I was lost in my memories hoping she would arrive before we were all handed our diplomas.

Chapter 3

"Hope, everyone's getting in their places. Let's go," Mr. Jones, the physical education teacher, shouted at everyone- including Hope.

Hope placed her cap on her head and adjusted the little tassel. She couldn't remember which side it went, so she glanced at the other students. She headed for her place. Still no sign of Katie.

Although my memories have edited parts of the past, it didn't all go smoothly. I resisted and tried everyone's patience just as any other child would do. I was met with punishment and consequences for my misbehavior as I demanded at times. Katie was fair with me and I felt a safety in the correction. I now know that children test their limits and demand correction as needed. This correction always lets them know their limits and provides a safe and secure feeling inside. Without it, difficulties occur.

The correction made me feel safe and loved, oddly enough. Katie was no coward and was not afraid of losing me. She wanted what was best for me and this included correction. Most parents in a divorce situation feel guilty and tend to not correct a child because they feel it would be harsh and cause the child more hurt. They also want the child to still 'like' them. When parents do this, they ignore a child's basic need for security.

Also, I was required to work for things I wanted so I felt a sense of responsibility and accomplishment. I was given daily chores. Since Katie and my dad had horses and other animals, there was plenty for me to do. Katie didn't coddle me just because I was in pain. She dealt with all areas of my development. She was kind when I needed kindness and firm when I needed firmness. She kept reminding me she was not perfect and made mistakes every day and didn't always know the right thing to do, but she was just doing her best to do the best for me. It felt more like a normal life- like a life without a divorce. Sometimes I loved that feeling even though I knew I would always have come from a divorce situation and still wanted my parents together- all of us together.

One day Katie was helping me get off to school in the morning. For reasons I didn't understand at the time, I dressed in clothes too small and inappropriate for me. Katie looked at me for a moment and I could tell she didn't know what to do. Then she blurted out, "I don't know if you are trying to 'find yourself' or you are intentionally trying to push my buttons to see if you can get a reaction from me *or* you need me to be *an adult and do an adult thing* and tell you that 'you are not leaving the house dressed like that.' Hope, I cannot tell you that I have time to sort this out right now, but I am going to do the adult thing. If I am making a mistake, I am sorry, but I want you to know I love you and care about you and this is what adults do when they love and care for a child. I am not ashamed of you and what people think of your father or me or you, I just want to let you know you are loved. No one would ignore this behavior." She rambled on and on.

She said these things almost apologetically, but the truth was that, deep inside I felt the love and was so glad that an adult did act like an adult and let me fell it. Without knowing it, she did the right thing for me at that time.

As the years went on, my love for Katie deepened. I still loved the time I spent with her. When I would see my mom, I spoke often of Katie. The more I talked about her to my mother and other relatives, the more they disliked her. Their reaction to her confused me. My mom and relatives called my friend 'weird.' They were concerned about how much time I spent with her. They said I shouldn't spend any time with her. They said bad things about Katie. I could not understand why they said these things. I was too young to realize they were jealous of her and how much I enjoyed her. They were threatened that I may want to spend time with Katie and not them.

In my mind Katie was the nicest person I had ever known. I enjoyed so much because of her. Now I was faced with the confusing fact that the most important people in my life hated her. How could they? I was so unprepared for their reaction. Didn't they know her the way I did? I wanted to please them, but I needed Katie. This caused so much more conflict inside me. I wanted to be loyal to my mother, but it was becoming clear to me that in order to do so, I would have to hate this new and wonderful friend I found.

Because of this, sometimes, when I was with Katie, I was quiet. I didn't respond the way I always used to. Eventually, I opened up and told her what was going around and around in my head. Also, I began to sabotage my fun when I was with Katie. I felt guilty when I caught myself having fun with her. I felt like my mom could see me and she would not approve. It didn't seem to matter that my dad liked Katie. He thought Katie did good things for me and with me. My mom insisted that I not relate to Katie.

People often asked if Katie was my mother. It caused me sadness when we said 'no' because many times I wished I was with my mother. I kept wishing she was at home with Dad and me. I wished my mom did all the things with me that Katie did. But sometimes the sadness was because secretly I wished Katie was my mother. I felt like a two-time loser. I lost my mother with the divorce and I was losing Katie to the jealousy.

I'm not sure if parents know that the hearts of their children really do belong to them. Deep inside of each child is the need to be loved and molded by the two adults given to them to do this. Yes, it is a big responsibility, but such a wonderful journey in life. To be the most important people to a child is beyond comprehension at times. Children really do listen to the words their parents speak about important issues like friends and successes and smoking and relationships, and well, *everything*. Parents should never neglect to talk to their children about everything. The children are counting on them.

I saw how upset my mother was when I spoke of Katie and our activities. My mom would promise to do the things Katie did and more. I began a new game. I would tell my mom what Katie and I were planning and then my mother would do that activity with me.

When I conveniently mentioned to my mother that Katie and I were going to plant flowers, she planted flowers with me. My mom took me swimming and skating and hiking each time I told her Katie was going to. My plan was working well. I was controlling my mom at the expense of my friendship with Katie. I was too young to see this was bad behavior. I just wanted time with my mom at any cost. I did not realize until many years later how my game hurt the people I loved.

Even though Katie knew what I was doing, she never rejected me. She knew why I did the things I did better than I did. I continued to spend time with her. Sometimes I would get lost in the fun we were having, and sometimes I couldn't enjoy my time with her. Katie just went with the flow, took all the minutes she could, and gave me the space I needed to sort things out. Looking back, I realize I lost precious moments of happy times I could have had to remember.

My family did not always act in my best interest. I was not being harmed by Katie. She was helping me like myself and helping me grow up. Her only motive was that I have a better life.

Sometimes I would catch myself acting like Katie. I knew this would be met with disapproval from my mother, so I changed my behavior.

I let others steal the happiness from my heart that Katie gave to me. She loved me unconditionally. She was not trying to be better than anyone else. My heart was definitely broken again.

After a while my games did not work anymore. There came a time when no one talked about my mom anymore. This was deadly for me. It was if she didn't exist when I was at my dad's. I was still consumed with wanting them back together and us being a normal and real family. I wanted to put them back together so I could put myself back together again. If they loved each other, I could believe they loved me too. Yet, I couldn't talk about my wants. I still really didn't know the words. I thought about both of them all the time. They moved on, I did not.

Katie often found me upstairs on my bed.

"I know you feel abandoned and the divorce tore your heart in many pieces, but life can still be good and you can still have happiness. You are not defective and you are lovable and worthy of good things. I am going to do whatever I can to help you see this," she said.

I said nothing.

"I know you are glad no one else notices. You want this to go away by itself. It doesn't work that way. We have to find a way to help you with all these confusing feelings," she continued.

Sometimes I wanted to hear what Katie would say and sometimes I just wanted to keep forgetting.

"It can't hurt forever, can it?" Katie asked.

I continued to say nothing, but thought to myself, *I think it can.*

Each student took their places. Music began playing. The dean of the college began organizing his podium for the upcoming events. Still no sign of Katie in the crowd.

Chapter 4

The dean asked all the guests to take their seats since commencement would be starting soon. He began to talk about the class preparing to graduate from their individual areas of study.

Again, my mind slipped back to my past. Things began changing at my dad's house. He began seeing a woman. Her name was Becky. My reaction was less than wonderful. He took her to dinner and bought her gifts. He sat next to her on the couch while they watched television together. I was so confused. He was supposed to love me best. He was supposed to spend time with me. In my mind I wanted him home waiting for me to come home from playing each evening. We always ate dinner together. The gifts he bought were supposed to be for me. What was going on?

I only wanted him to be nice to me. I saw her as the enemy. She was trying so hard to be nice to me and have me accept her. That was not happening. I felt an overwhelming need to protect my mother's position in this house. It wasn't as if my mother had been in this house in many years, but still, this is what I was sure was going to happen again one day. I wanted to keep everything the same as when my mom was home.

Anyway, I was elevated to the status of wife a long time ago and was not about to be demoted now. I was the woman of the house and intended to have it stay that way. I knew my 'place' in this house and it was not the same 'place' Becky thought it should be.

Since my mother always told me that divorced children always try to break up their parents' relationships, I knew I had her blessing on the matter. In fact, she even fueled my fire. She never intended to come home to Dad and me, but she wanted him to be waiting for her. This unfortunate obsession with splitting my dad and Becky up only added to my lost childhood. I spent time trying to split my dad up with Becky instead of being a child. My dad pretended not to notice my behavior. He never said anything. It was my mother who compelled me to this behavior instead of acceptance.

All my friends told me not to worry. They said my dad loved me more than anything and Becky might even go away. This relationship seemed serious though. Becky was trying to be very nice to me and sometimes I felt guilty trying to get rid of her. How could my father do this to my mother and me? We had been waiting for mom to come home. Even if Dad had given up and moved on, I had not. I failed to enjoy or appreciate all the good things about Becky. I never saw her as generous, creative, and a good addition to our family. I never saw her as someone who made my dad happy. I just saw her as an intruder with no business to be here at all. It would be many years before I realized I could have loved more than one person at a time and still really loved and respected my mother.

I needed my dad to love my mom and no one else. This would be ideal because this was the normal course of events in life. This new situation was too much for me to handle. How could my mom come back if Becky was here? They would just fight.

I tried every way I could to separate them. Since I was young, I felt powerless. I tried to get the adults to help me. I discovered that adults will react if I tap into their emotions regarding my well-being and safety. It didn't matter to me if I was not telling the truth about things. I just had a mission to get my own way and serve my own purposes. I had the impression that grown-ups were big and more powerful than I. The feeling of being powerless led me to try to control these two people from hurting me more after this divorce.

Dad and Becky began making changes in the house. They did this because they were starting a new life together. It was natural, but my reaction surprised everyone.

The first change Dad and Becky wanted to make was to send pictures of me to my mom's. He picked pictures of me with my mom to send. I reacted terribly. I wanted everything to stay the same and that meant no changes of any kind. Katie saw how I reacted and how emotional I became. I was frantic. I started pulling the pictures out of everyone's hands and put them back into the book Dad always kept them in. I could not express myself. I still didn't know the words. Everyone was stunned. I replaced all the pictures. I put them where they belonged. It didn't matter that Katie told me that my mother wanted the pictures so she could share them with me.

It seemed to me that the adults thought I had forgotten about the divorce after so many years, but it was obviously still affecting me. I picked a picture to put on my dresser. Of all the pictures to choose from, the one I picked was the picture of my mom and dad on their wedding day. I was sending a clear message to everyone and anyone willing to listen.

When I looked at Dad with Becky, he seemed so happy. I wanted him to be happy. Unfortunately, I wanted him to be happy with my mom and not Becky.

Because of my unexpected reaction to all the new situations I was facing, the grown-ups made me live through new tortures. It was obvious to them that I had unresolved issues about the divorce that happened many years before. The first torture was the videos. I sat there not knowing what to expect. The videos dealt with divorce and feelings children may experience as a result- and on and on it went. I didn't want to sit and watch them. The truth was I did not want to accept the divorce and I wanted to pretend that none of this had ever happened. All would be fixed if my mom would just come home.

Next were the books. They did not help either. I wasn't open to this information at this time. There wasn't anything wrong with the information, things inside of me were not well. I remember sitting and wishing for it all to be over. Katie could tell I just wanted to retreat to my room with my private wishes and dreams.

Then I had to live through family conferences. They were the worst. Dad, Becky, and Katie would have little talks with me. More than ever I wished I was invisible. Dad would say the words that dealt the most devastating emotional blow- he didn't love my mom anymore and she was never coming back. I would get a very sad look on my face and begin to cry. How could anyone be so cruel?

When they asked if I understood, I just nodded. I nodded my head 'yes' because I knew this was the answer they wanted to hear. If I said 'yes,' then they would leave me alone. I never felt they wanted to hear the truth about me or how I felt. I didn't even want to feel my real feelings. I went to my room and cried in private, where no one could see or know the real me.

When Katie came to comfort me, I just turned to the wall as she rubbed my back. I was so disappointed. Why didn't my dad miss my mom the way I did? I would never give up wanting them back together again. I could not tell them that. They would not approve. They would just keep trying to 'fix' me. I made other girlfriends go away, why couldn't I make this one go away?

Becky, on the other hand was relentless. She tried so hard to be nice to me. The harder she tried, the more I refused to be nice back. I had to be subtle about it though, my dad told Becky that I liked her. Becky, Katie, and I knew I didn't, but my games worked. I always looked like the good guy and Becky always looked like she was jealous of me and trying to fit in where she didn't belong.

Since Becky practically lived with us soon after her and dad starting seeing each other, she tried to act like my mom. Step mom is what they called her. I called her step monster. She packed lunch for me. I took the lunch, but when I arrived home, I told her I forgot I brought a lunch so I charged lunch at the cafeteria. She bought me earrings once and I told her I lost one on the way home from school. She was not getting the message. When she bought me a special stamp with my name on it, I left it where the puppy could get it and chew it so you couldn't even read my name.

Most people talked badly about her anyway. They said she was not a real mom and was weird for pretending to be one. Katie thought it was wonderful how she wanted me to know she cared about me. Katie was always trying to make the bad things good. Not this time. I hid my true feelings. I just looked like a normal child who lost things and had a dog that damaged things. The funny thing was that they never seemed to notice that my mom's gifts were never ruined.

Becky tried to include me in everything from decorating for holidays to cleaning house and planting flowers.

"I plant flowers with my mother at my mother's house," I told her.

"Well, you're here now. You can plant at both houses I think. Have some fun and enjoy life at your dad's too," Becky insisted.

I didn't want Becky to think she could take my mom's place. I had a mom and didn't need another one. She was not my dad's wife, she was just a girlfriend.

Becky tried to take pictures of me and start a scrapbook of 'Hope's Memories at Dad's' she called it. I told her I did that at my mom's. Even if I didn't, I said it anyway.

Sometimes I felt guilty hating her. It wasn't her fault my parents divorced. Becky bought me a very pretty outfit once. I would have looked badly if I refused to wear it, so when I did wear it and arrived home from school, I showed her the spaghetti sauce I spilled all over it at lunchtime. Her face was puzzled, but we both knew I could never wear that outfit again.

My message was one of total rejection. I wanted her to go away and live in another house. She was not my mother and I did not intend to listen to her rules or be nice to her. Everyone agreed with me.

While riding in the car, I made sure I sat in the middle, next to my dad. I wished Becky wasn't even in the car. I talked to my dad as if she wasn't there. I talked about the things we did before Becky came along and implied we didn't need her.

Becky would bring up my behavior to my dad. When she did this, they argued. Dad told Becky she was wrong. He told her to ignore the things I did and to grow up. I hoped their fighting would make her go away. Dad didn't seem to want to hear about it or be bothered with this. He acted like it didn't affect him. My plan was to get them to stop being together. I wanted my plan to work.

Since my mom didn't like Becky, she also tried to have my dad atop seeing her. I now know the adults in my life were not mature in the way they handled the divorce. They each needed to let the other go on with their lives. They kept pretending they were still married and had something to say about the other. I was caught in the middle of the games and jealousy. I was only a child who never should have been put in this position. My own issues were enough for me to deal with.

Dad continued to love Becky. I was devastated. How could he do this? This was the worst thing I could have imagined. All the games I tried did not work out the way I had hoped and anticipated. I tried to hurt my father by deciding to move to my mother's.

The votes were in. Everyone said Dad should have picked me and not Becky. He didn't want to be forced to make a decision like this by a child. I lost a war I was so sure I could never lose. Actually, no one wins in this situation. I certainly did not win. Becky did not win, she felt terrible. My dad did not win. Deep inside he also felt terrible. He was torn apart.

Katie felt there were too many games played between immature adults with a child in the middle.

Chapter 5

My confusion went from bad to worse. Since I made the decision to live at my mom's I went through with it. Life at my mom's was filled with high expectations. She had promised to be everything my heart thought my mom should and would be. She promised we would do all the things Katie and I did. Lots of promises - or should I say, lots of broken promises.

I took all my belongings from my dad's to my mom's. I wanted to recreate my life there. This was not possible and did not happen. I began to miss the life I had at Dad's, but my hurt took a new turn. When I was at my mom's, I missed my dad, but when I was at my dad's, I missed my mom. It was confusing to have two sets of rules and two sets of routines. I had to adjust every time I went somewhere. I had a deep need to feel I was wanted somewhere. I needed to feel I was wanted at both houses. I wanted to know they both still loved me and wanted me. I still could not speak and I could not tell them what I needed. Sometimes I didn't even know how to make sense of the jumbled feelings inside of me anyway. My silence made everyone think I was okay inside.

Since there were other children at my mom's I saw her with them. I watched her love them and wondered if she still loved me. I not only wondered if she still loved me, but if she still loved me best. When children fight amongst themselves, parents usually defend their own children - and the whole big blended family mess begins all over again. This is how it went at Mom's. The adults never seem to see the children as the instigators of the conflict. The adults were drawn into the conflict without realizing the negative ramifications of their actions in response to the children.

I really liked the attention I received when I would go from house to house at times. I was treated like a new guest for a while and then, when everyone went back to their usual routines, I would change locations again.

It's easy to get people to focus on other things instead of my pain because they didn't notice my pain. Since I didn't say anything, they thought I was just fine. I didn't stay any one place long enough for anyone to catch on to what went on inside of me.

Katie could see that I was insecure and needed more attention because of this insecurity. I was always off balance emotionally by this constant conflict and didn't know how to make it go away. Nothing felt settled in my life. I felt I had to take care of my dad because he had no one. I felt this way even though Becky was there. I needed him to need me. I wanted to be with my mom too. I felt split right down the middle. Big person decisions should be left to big people. I was more disturbed by all these decisions I made to move around and such.

Adults should have made these decisions. I think it would have helped me feel more secure.

Sometimes, when I was alone, I thought about the things Katie and I talked about, but things were still confusing to me. I wish mom and dad would live alone or with me and not with some other man or woman. When you're little, none of these things make sense.

It takes a long time to grow up and see things more clearly. I didn't want them to be alone, but I also didn't want them to be with strangers. All my friends said the same thing.

46

Chapter 6

The Dean had moved on in the events of graduation. He introduced the speaker for today. As he took the microphone, he began a speech to inspire all the graduates to be all they could be.

I was spending much of my time now going back and forth from my mom's to my dad's house. Becky was still at my dad's and they seemed quite comfortable in their routine. I was still trying to split them up. It didn't matter who it was, any woman would spark the same reaction in me, it just happened to be Becky now.

I was older now and more determined now. I would show her my place here. I was still convinced I was elevated to the status of the wife and would do all the things a wife would do.

I saw how it irritated Becky when I wore my father's clothing. He reminded Becky that even she wore his clothes at times. When I decorated the house, he told Becky not to let those things bother her. He told her I was just trying to help out.

I left my clothes everywhere since it was really my house. When Becky complained about my behavior, my dad told her she was picking on me. The truth was that my real mom told me to pick up clothes also. Becky was doing exactly what any normal adult would do. It was like we were all choosing sides for the war and my dad I were on one side and Becky was all alone on her side.

Since I owned everything in the house, I left my wash in the wash machine in an attempt to prevent anyone else- Becky really- from using the washer. This again infuriated her. My mission accomplished.

I possessed every room in the house too. I placed my bathroom supplies over the counter in the bathroom and on the shelves. There was no room for any of Becky's things. I made sure of that. The kitchen was also mine and I decided where the dishes and pots and pans were placed.

I wanted Becky to know she was not needed. I could cook and clean now. I made my dad's favorite cakes and cookies. I wanted Becky to know that I was all my dad needed. We had a great life before she came along.

I decorated the shelves and picked the curtains. If Becky did something in the house, I undid it and re-did it my way. I wanted her to know I was the woman of the house, she was not. When Becky talked to Dad about my behavior, again he said she just overreacting and just jealous of me. He told her I was just helping. My plan worked well. They fought often and furiously about me. I just sat quietly and let it happen.

When Becky complained about me, everyone agreed she was jealous of me and was the 'bad' guy because I was just a child. They saw me as harmless and her as the outsider. I liked it this way. People would say that my parents should always pick me over the adult in their lives. They also said that whatever I did should be defended. I am old enough now to know better. I knew my behavior was wrong and as long as no one forced me to behave differently, I didn't. I enjoyed people coming to my defense.

My behavior prompted many discussions in the house. The discussion of who was the adult woman and who was the child came up. Who was the girlfriend/wife and who was the daughter? How were the two supposed to act and interact with the man involved with both of them? The issue of who was the "woman" of the house also came up. Children do not buy and maintain houses, so what would make me think I was the 'woman' of the house and was to do the adult woman activities? Who lived with whom? Did I live with Dad and Becky, or did Becky live with Dad and me? There were issues about adult-to-adult relationships v. adult-to-child relationships. Adult-to-adult relationships take maturity on the part of adults and sometimes adults avoid this and feel it easier to concentrate on the adult-to-child relationship. These appear to be easier for some adults to engage in.

I once overheard a conversation between Becky and Katie. Becky often confided in her. "I am having a very difficult time with Hope, sometimes Katie. It seems like her dad sticks up for her disruptive behavior and it causes friction in our relationship"

"Yes, I see that this upsets you, Becky. What do you think you should do about it?" Katie asked.

"I'm at the end of my rope. If something doesn't make sense here soon, I may pack and leave," Becky replied.

Those were the words I was waiting to hear. Then Katie interrupted my happiness to say something profound again and mess up my plans.

"Well, Becky, I want to share with you a little nursery rhyme. The one that goes:

> *Pussy-cat, pussy-cat,*
> *where have you been?*
> *I've been to England to see the Queen.*
>
> *Pussy-cat, pussy-cat,*
> *what saw you there?*
> *I saw a mouse run under her chair.*

"Becky, I know this sounds silly, but this cat was in the presence of splendor and royalty and such, and all it noticed was an insignificant mouse run under the chair-not what one would expect to comment on. I learned a long time ago that sometimes the little things distract us from the really important things. Whether a child dresses inappropriately or has a disrespectful mouth or acts out or tries to control a household- or just about anything, it is often a sign of real hurts that are real deep. People see the 'insignificant' behavior instead of the really important hurts in the child.

"Hope really does have a broken heart and the issues are deep. The behavior we see sometimes has two possible purposes. One, is to hide the pain that is very big and very deep inside and have attention diverted elsewhere. Two, is to push your buttons and cause a reaction to have her desired fantasy world where she is not hurt and her mom and dad do reconcile. Either way, I think sometimes if we take a different look at things, we can manage to tolerate them better. Don't get off the real issues is all I'm trying to say.

"Children can only act like children. I know this sounds silly, but they are not adults. They cannot be expected to cope and reason like adults because they are not. This is the job of the adults in the child's life. Hope is only being what she is capable of being at the present time. Hopefully, this can and will change."

"Thanks, Katie. I know she's hurt. It gets clouded by all the extra frenzy that goes on in the house sometimes. I'll keep all that in mind," Becky responded.

There was one kind thing I still remember Becky saying to a friend. While she was on the phone, she said she felt she could use her 'muscle' to win this war and squish me like a bug, but that would be cruel and would not make her feel good. I knew she was stronger and smarter and more able to sort things out in life. She was an adult, I was just a child. She said she wanted to be with my dad, but not at the expense of my fragile heart and mind. She really could see how much I struggled. No one knew what to do at times with my hurts.

Katie asked Dad if he was afraid to address the problems because he felt helpless to help me with these problems. She also asked if he was afraid I would leave and never come back if he didn't give into my every whim.

Dad said sometimes he felt guilty that it was his fault I hurt. He felt this way because the marriage didn't work between my mother and him. He hoped it would just sort itself out.

It seemed to me the extent of my anger and my acting out and the hatred I displayed was directly proportional to the amount of hurt I had experienced and the insecurity I felt. I referred to it as creative hatred.

All my confusion and bad behavior accomplished for me was more torture. It was worse than the conferences and the videos and books. They decided I needed a counselor. My dad was too embarrassed to take me to the counselor. Feelings were not what he was good at expressing. Becky was out of the question because she was basically the enemy and the need for me to have counseling. That left Katie. She was elected to take me.

As Katie took me to the counseling appointment, she tried to explain they were all just concerned about me. I was silent and just dreaded this. I felt like such a problem to everyone.

Katie explained to the counselor that everyone thought I had some issues about my parents' divorce and abandonment concerns and low self-esteem. She proceeded to tell the counselor all the variety of things I had been doing. Katie talked as though I wasn't sitting there. She told that counselor everything. Then she informed the counselor that I was very hurt and very clever at switching the subject off myself and on to something else to avoid my inner pain. Katie also told her that I was prone to exaggerate the truth to encourage emotional reaction to also divert the attention off my hurting heart to a different subject. The counselor just listened and then Katie left.

As I talked to the counselor, she asked if I realized my parents were not going to get back together again.

I remember as I sat there in the counselor's office, for a moment I really wanted to say what I thought and what I was feeling. What I really wanted to do was stand up and scream and wave my hands emphatically and tell her, "MY NAME IS

HOPE AND MY PARENTS WERE DIVORCED WHEN I WAS VERY YOUNG. I AM ANGRY AND HURT AND CONFUSED AND I HATE THAT THEY DID THIS TO ME. THEY SHOULD HAVE TALKED AND THEY SHOULD HAVE LISTENED TO EACH OTHER AND MADE THINGS HAPPY IN OUR LIVES. I CANNOT CONCENTRATE ON NORMAL THINGS SOMETIMES BECAUSE I FEEL LIKE THEY BOTH ABANDONED ME AND DID NOT CARE ABOUT MY FEELINGS. EVERY DAY I FEEL LIKE THEY WILL ABANDON ME AGAIN. MY LIFE IS BROKEN AND I DON'T KNOW HOW TO SORT OUT THE FEELINGS I HAVE. THEY BRING OTHER PEOPLE INTO OUR LIVES WHO SOMETIMES STAY AND SOMETIMES GO. I DON'T KNOW HOW TO FEEL ABOUT THESE PEOPLE BECAUSE I HAVE SO MUCH CONFLICT ABOUT THEM BEING HERE. I FEEL DEFECTIVE AND UNLOVABLE. I FEEL NO ONE UNDERSTANDS THE DEPTH OF THE HURT THAT HAPPENED TO ME WHEN THEY SPLIT UP. EVERY DAY I TRY TO IMAGINE WHAT IT WOULD BE LIKE TO FEEL NORMAL!" There were so many things I wanted to say straight from the depths of my heart, but....

I did my usual. I said what she wanted to hear. I nodded and said I understood the two most important people in my life were never going to get back together. It was like a knife pierced my heart and no one understood what it felt like to be forced to say the words I wished I never had to say. After, she moved on. She did not seem to realize I was only avoiding addressing my inner issues. She seemed content to have 'solved' some part of my 'problem.'

She did not pry into the depths of my broken heart to expose all the pain and disappointment there. She was easy to figure out how to hide my true self from. I had her off the track faster than any other person I had encountered. My inability to concentrate and my delays in growth and development emotionally were never issues she addressed. We never talked about my behavior and the reasons I behaved these ways. We talked about unrelated topics.

The counselor discussed everything with Katie. She told Katie I was accepting of the divorce and the real issues were much different than she was presented. The counselor also told Katie that she usually tells stepparents to 'butt out' when it comes to the children.

"Butt out?" Katie was puzzled. "You tell stepparents to 'butt out'? I don't get it. That woman cooks, cleans, helps pay bills, shares her life with Hope's dad, washes clothes, and many other things. But when the 'rubber meets the road,' you're saying she's not the 'real' mother or the 'real' wife, she's the real fake who has no business there anyway. Sometimes I think the only thing Becky should be butting out of is the whole situation altogether. Relationships and parenting are difficult enough without adding these pitfalls to the package. Tell me, how come Hope has to respect teachers and librarians who are not her mother, but even though Becky is an adult, she doesn't count? The world treats stepparents like freaks instead of the wonderful people who step in when they don't have to - who step in when someone else stepped out?"

The counselor looked like she didn't get any of it. She looked at Katie like she was from another planet. Maybe these things never occurred to her. I got it all, but still didn't feel like I had the tools to deal with all that was inside of me. I knew I had to deal with these things or they would deal with me my entire life, but I just wasn't quite ready. I said nothing all the way home.

Chapter 7

After the speaker finished, one of the students came to the microphone and began to sing the song, "The Theme from Mahogany" by Diana Ross. As she sang, "*Do you know where you're going to? Do you like the things that life is showing you?*" I still did not see Katie.

Many years have come and gone since that day at the counselor's. Katie and I spent time together on occasion. My dad stayed with Becky and they married. My mom never did come back, but I had arrived at many important conclusions. Thanks to Katie and all the patient people I had on my life, my life did go well. Katie was there every time I called and needed steering on the right direction. She showed that there's always hope. My family and friends did show me unconditional love in my life. I had many hurts, but had much support in my life to overcome them.

The constant turmoil I felt as a child has gone. My heart is quiet and I realize I have many good things that made up for this imperfect life I lived. I have learned that other children are challenged with many things in life as well as I was. Some children have childhood diseases or the death of one or both parents to deal with. Some children grow up in great poverty as well as many other challenges all around us. My parents are imperfect people and I live in an imperfect world. Everyone did the best they could. They meant me no harm.

I know they love me and I love them and all the people that have come into my life to make it better. It is possible to love more than one person and see all the good in the people who come into our lives.

I can cope. I can like myself. I can see myself as lovable. I can think good thoughts about my future. I know nothing was my fault and I could never have changed all the bad events of my life, but they could turn into something that made me stronger and better as a person.

I can make good decisions about relationships and now know that good things can happen to me in my life.

I can stop the behavior that only hurts myself and the people I really do love.

I have learned to talk about my feelings. I now see what I think and feel as important and valuable. I know there are resources in the world to help struggling individuals sort issues out.

I am a valuable person who is loved.

I have learned that many people 'curse the darkness,' but forbid anyone to 'light a candle.' I have chosen to light many candles in my life. The truth is so much better than the lies I told myself.

Katie helped me when I did not know how to help myself. There was another nursery rhyme she loved- Humpty Dumpty. She said that when he fell off the wall and had a great fall, all the king's horses and all the king's men couldn't put him together again. Katie said this was like us in life. Sometimes we fall off the wall. Sometimes we have a great fall. We need someone to put us back together again. We need someone to help probe into the deep parts of our hearts when we feel shattered inside. She assured me that, unlike

Humpty, I could be fixed. When I opened up and my pain was revealed, that there would be a way to put me back together again. All fixed. She promised.

I know I can love myself for who I am and not let the past hurts prevent me from being the person I can be.

I have had the rare privilege of seeing many lives. Of seeing many roads to choose. Katie blessed me with the words of Robert Frost. She could recite his poem by heart. "Two roads diverged in a yellow wood, and be one traveler, long I stood... I took the road less traveled by, and..." this really has made all the difference. Today was a day I could say I chose the road less traveled by. The path to healing and wellness is sometimes a long and difficult one, but "it has made all the difference." It was worth it. Healing for my broken heart made it possible for me to graduate today with my teaching degree.

I was blessed to have all the people I had in my life to make it a better one. I have come to know that the only way to true happiness and healing is to forgive the ones who hurt me so much and sort out the painful issues. This was the true road to freedom from the hurts of the past.

When divorce happens, kids do suffer. It is not fatal. The issues are important, but the behavior needs to be understood and gentle is a word for the matter. At the end of the day, it will not matter where the dishes are kept and stacked and who wears whose clothes-the hearts of the little ones trying to sort things out and not blaming themselves are what is truly important. Children should be about the business of being children.

Care for each other talk to each other get through it all together.

I asked Katie once if I was worth it. She hugged me very hard and said, "Yes, my little girl, you were worth it."

Just where was Katie? They had already started calling students' names and giving diplomas. My turn was coming. I was wringing my hands as I continued to scan the audience. I looked down to watch my step as they were just about to call my name. When I looked up, there she was. She had just arrived and was standing in the back. There were no more seats. My Katie. We shared so many childhood memories. She was the one who believed in me when I was unable to believe in myself. She was the one who had seen the hurt and walked with me through it. She gave me my childhood back. She helped me with the difficult issues and I wanted her to be proud of me this day. As I saw the smile on her face as I received my diploma, I knew she was.

The End

www.ingramcontent.com/pod-product-compliance
Lightning Source LLC
Chambersburg PA
CBHW021158080526
44588CB00008B/406